LET'S-READ-AND-FIND-OUT BOOK CLUB EDITION

Birds at Night

by ROMA GANS
Illustrated by ALIKI

THOMAS Y. CROWELL COMPANY   **NEW YORK**

Early in the morning birds eat as much as they can. They eat nearly all day long. In the evening they eat a lot again. As soon as it's dark the birds go to sleep.

1

Some fly to a woods and stay there
from sundown to sunrise. Many sleep
in leafy bushes, in vines, and in trees.
The bushes and vines shelter the birds
from storms and keep them safe from
owls and cats.

Swallows sleep high up inside barns.

Starlings roost side by side under bridges. Phoebes perch under the eaves of buildings. Ducks and swans often sleep while floating on the water. They sleep a while, wake and eat, and then sleep again. Sometimes snapping turtles catch them while they are asleep.

In the daytime a bird often sits
quietly. The bird's eyes seem to be
closed. But the bird is not sleeping. It
is only resting.

Birds have three eyelids. They have upper lids, lower lids, and blinkers. They use only the blinkers when they rest. Blinkers clean the eyes and keep them moist. Birds can see through them. They can see a cat even when their eyes seem to be closed.

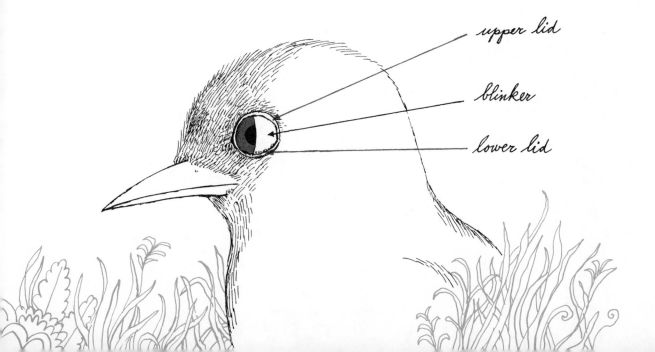

upper lid

blinker

lower lid

At night, when birds sleep, they shut both the upper and lower lids. Now they cannot see their enemies. But they are safe from cats and owls in trees or bushes or other shelters.

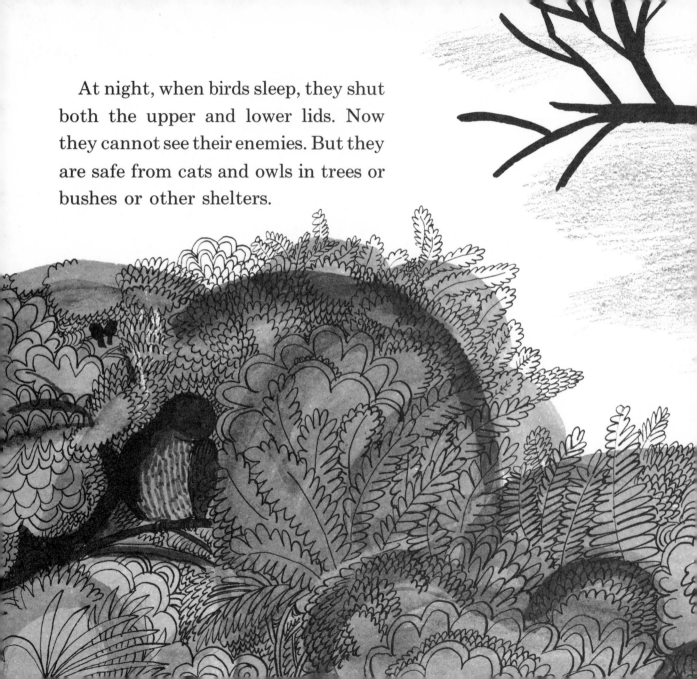

Many birds clamp their feet to branches when they sleep. A big muscle in each leg locks the bird's feet to the branch. This keeps the bird from falling off. When the bird wants to fly again it unlocks the leg muscle by standing up straight.

Long-legged birds like geese and herons sometimes sleep while standing on one leg. Woodpeckers hook their claws into the bark of a tree and sleep. They look as if they had stopped to rest while climbing up a tree.

Birds have high body temperatures. Their bodies are warmer than yours. Your temperature is about 98.6 degrees; a bird's is about 106 degrees. The hummingbird has the highest temperature of all. Its temperature can go to 113 degrees.

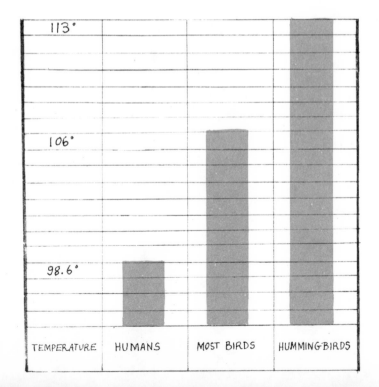

| TEMPERATURE | HUMANS | MOST BIRDS | HUMMINGBIRDS |

113°

106°

98.6°

Birds must eat a lot to keep their bodies so warm. When they rest or sleep they stop eating. Then their temperature drops lower. On cold days they need to eat more than on warm days.

When winter comes and days get colder many birds fly to warm places. Others stay where the winters are very cold. But they must keep warm in order to stay alive.

On a cold day you wear boots to keep your feet warm. You wear mittens and a sweater and a heavy coat. At night you sleep under warm blankets. Birds have no boots, no mittens, no sweater or blanket. How do they keep warm?

Just before it grows dark birds eat all they can. They need a lot of food to keep them warm through the night. Their feathers hold in the heat.

Feathers are very light. All the feathers of a big bird would weigh only as much as fifteen pennies.

Feathers are very light, but they keep birds warm. Each feather has a strong shaft from tip to end. On each side of the shaft are little "hairs," or barbs. They are locked together by tiny hooks called barbules. They are like a zipper. The barbs lock together so the feathers are airtight. Wind cannot blow through feathers.

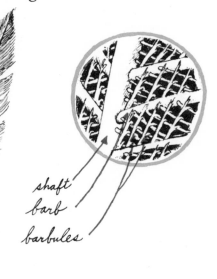

shaft
barb
barbules

body feather

down feather

flight feather

The feathers lie one over the other. They overlap like shingles on a roof. All together they make an airtight wind jacket.

The wind may blow the feathers so
they stick up. Then the bird shakes
itself. Each feather falls back in place.
Again the bird's covering is airtight.

Most birds have an oil gland on the back near the tail. With its beak the bird takes oil from the gland and rubs the oil over its feathers. The oil makes the feathers waterproof. Heavy rain cannot soak through the bird's airtight covering. Under its feathers on cold, wet days and nights the bird keeps warm and dry.

Under the airtight feathers is a layer of soft small feathers called down. Birds fluff up the layer of down with air. The layer of down and air is like a soft blanket. When the down is puffed up under the outer feathers it makes the bird round like a ball of feathers. The air in the layer of down is kept warm by the bird's body.

As soon as they wake in the morning, birds eat as much as they can. They need a lot of food because they use it up very fast as they fly about.

28

Birds cannot always find enough food to stay alive. We can help birds by feeding them. They need bread crumbs, seeds, and suet, especially in cold weather.

30

Food makes the heat that keeps a bird warm. The layer of down with its cover of airtight feathers holds in the heat. Birds stay warm even on the coldest days when they are flying and on the coldest nights when they are sleeping.

ABOUT THE AUTHOR

Roma Gans has called children "enlightened, excited citizens." She believes in the fundamental theory that children are eager to learn and will whet their own intellectual curiosity if they are encouraged by and provided with stimulating teachers and materials.

Dr. Gans received her B.S. from Columbia Teachers College and her Ph.D. from Columbia University. She began her work in the educational field in the public schools of the Middle West as a teacher, supervisor, and assistant superintendent of schools. She is Professor Emeritus of Childhood Education at Teachers College, Columbia University, and lectures extensively throughout this country and Canada.

Dr. Gans is vitally interested in nature and all its phenomena. She has many bird-feeding stations at her house in West Redding, Connecticut, where she watches birds and their habits. She enjoys living in the country where she can observe the changing seasons of the year.

ABOUT THE ARTIST

Versatility is the key to Aliki's career as a commercial artist and a children's book author and illustrator. Besides her art work, she loves music, books, and making dolls.

Aliki grew up in Philadelphia, where she attended the Museum College of Art. Here extensive European travels have included a four-year motor and painting tour through Italy, Yugoslavia, and Greece. In private life, Aliki is Mrs. Franz Brandenberg. She and her husband and their two children live in New York City.